THIS JOURNAL BELONGS TO:

What is a Gratitude Journal?

HAVE YOU EVER HEARD THE EXPRESSION: "COUNT YOUR BLESSINGS"? - YOU DEFINITELY SHOULD DO! GRATITUDE JOURNAL IS A PRACTICAL EXERCISE OF REFLECTING ON AND WRITING DOWN THE THINGS YOU ARE THANKFUL FOR ON A REGULAR BASIS. THIS WAY, YOU CAN FOCUS MORE ON THE POSITIVE ASPECTS OF YOUR LIFE, SO IT BALANCES OUT THE NEGATIVITY. KEEPING A GRATITUDE DIARY IS A POPULAR PRACTICE IN POSITIVE PSYCHOLOGY AND IT IS AIMED TO TEACH YOU APPRECIATE LITTLE JOYS, DEVELOP OBSERVATION, EXPRESS CLEARLY YOUR THOUGHTS, IMPROVE WRITING SKILLS, BUILD A STRONGER, CONFIDENT PERSONALITY.

READY TO ROCK IT?

Why am I here?

TO START YOU OFF, ASK YOURSELF THESE 3 SIMPLE QUESTIONS:

1. HOW DO I UNDERSTAND THE WORD <u>GRATITUDE</u>?
2. IS IT MY <u>DECISION</u> TO WRITE A JOURNAL OR SOMEONE ELSE'S SUGGESTION?
3. ONE MAIN <u>GOAL</u> I WOULD LIKE TO REACH BY STARTING THIS PRACTICE?

P.S. YOU CAN GO INTO DETAILS, BUT KEEP IT SIMPLE, WE ARE NOT WRITING ESSAY EXAMS HERE :)

Dear Friend,

This journal is aimed to help you in practicing gratitude in all it's meanings. As we didn't want your journey to be boring, we decided to give you as much flexibility as possible, so we made the journal undated with a decent amount of lines to write. You are free to put down the date at the beginning of your notes and it's not a must to do it daily, if you don't feel like. The notebook is filled with prompts, advices, interesting facts, coloring pages and quizzes.

Enjoy!

Your path begins here

The first step towards getting somewhere is to decide you're not going to stay where you are.

J.P. Morgan

Did you know?

64% of American adults currently consume
coffee every day.
Britons are believed to drink around 165million
cups of tea, this compares to 95million cups of
coffee – quite a gap.

What do you prefer

Useful Habits

Wake Up Early!

TOP BENEFITS:
- IMPROVED COGNITIVE FUNCTION.
- BETTER SLEEP QUALITY.
- EXTRA TIME TO EAT BREAKFAST.
- TIME FOR MORNING WORKOUTS.
- BETTER MOOD AND MENTAL HEALTH.
- REDUCES STRESS.
- INCREASES ORGANIZATION AND PRODUCTIVITY.
- PEACEFUL MORNINGS

Relaxing Coloring Page

"Harry Potter" Quiz:

1.Name Harry Potter's parents
2.Which actor played the character Cedric Diggory?
3.What creature is Aragog?
4.Who were the four founders of Hogwarts?
5.What spell would you use to light the tip of your wand?

Can you find the way out?

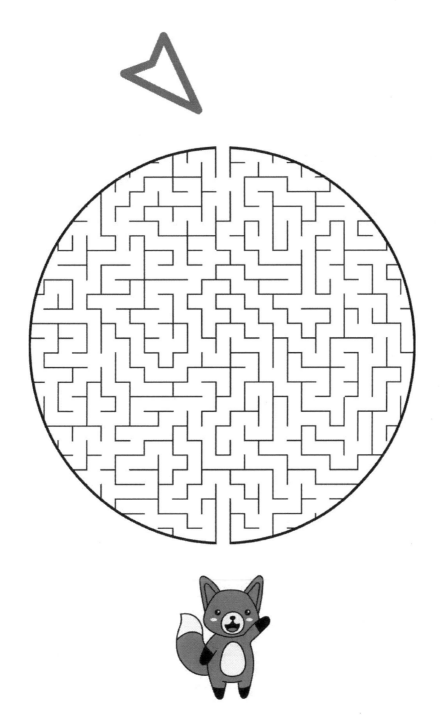

Want to make a difference?

Kindness ideas

Buy some pet food and drop it off
at a local animal centre.

REFLECTIONS

over last days, weeks, months

Mood:

Today I am proud of....

....

....

....

Goals for the next 30 days:

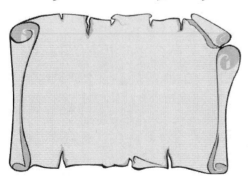

My picture

Next
section

As long as you keep going, you'll keep getting better. And as you get better, you gain more confidence. That alone is success.

Tamara Taylor

Did you know?

One-third of adults still sleep with
a comfort object.
Do you also have one? :)

Useful Habits

START YOUR MORNING WITH A POSITIVE EMOTION

1.In your morning routine, leave a little time for make up, dress up + accessories and your favorite perfume of course

2.Wish Good Luck to yourself! Before heading to work, school and during the day wish yourself good luck and compliment yourself. Listen to positive affirmations, which long term will bring good results.

3.Celebrate victories - big and small. Even if you didn't achieve the desired result straightaway, appreciate yourself for what you've learned and managed to do so far.

Relaxing Coloring Page

"Matrix" quiz:

1. Thomas Anderson is the real name of which character in The Matrix?

2. A mysterious message on his computer urges Neo to follow which animal?

3. In The Matrix Reloaded, Neo visits the last city left in the real world. What's its name?

4. Which piece of technology do awakened humans use to exit the Matrix from inside?

5. For what reason is it revealed the machines require farms of humans?

Can you solve a
Sudoku?

9				4	6			8
		8					5		7
1				3	5			6
			1		9	6		
	5			7			8	
		3	5		4			
8			2	9				5
7		6				3		
5			6	1			2	

Want to make a difference?

Kindness ideas

Compliment a business on their customer service

REFLECTIONS

over last
days, weeks, months

Mood tracking:

Joyful - orange
Happy - pink
Indifferent - yellow
Sad - green
Angry - Grey

Today I am proud of:

. . . .
. . . .
. . . .
. . . .
. . . .
. . . .

Sleep 7-8 h every day

Give up on a bad habit   Try a fitness challenge

Pick a Challenge

Learn a new language   Meditate daily

Read 20 pages a day

KEEP
ON
GOING

Only I can change my life.
No one can do it for me.

Carol Burnett

Useful Habits

Drink Plenty of Water

Key Benefits:

1.carrying nutrients and oxygen to your cells
2.flushing bacteria from your bladder
3.aiding digestion
4.normalizing blood pressure
5.stabilizing the heartbeat

Relaxing Coloring

"Game of Thrones" Quiz:

1. What is the name of Jon's direwolf?
2. What is the main religion of the Seven Kingdoms?
3. In the first episode, King Robert Baratheon says "In my dreams, I kill him every night." To whom is the King referring and why?
4. Why could Jon leave the Night's Watch, since his vows were for life?
5. What is the name of Arya Stark's sword?

Ready for brain teaser questions?

1. 84% of people reading this will not find the the mistake in this A,B,C,D,E,F,G,H,I,J,K,L,M,N,O,P,Q,R,S,T,U, V,W,X,Y,Z.

2. What flies without wings?

3. What five letter word becomes shorter when you add two letters to it?

4.What can you keep but cannot share and once you share it, you can't keep it anymore?

5.What call for help, when written in capital letters, is the same forwards, backwards and upside down?

Want to make a difference?

Kindness ideas

Help someone who is lost

BRAVO

REFLECTIONS

over last
days, weeks, months

Challenges I've overcome

....
....
....
....

Mood Tracker:

Try drawing your daily little joy
(ex. cup of coffee)

You are doing GREAT!

Look
HOW FAR YOU'VE COME!

GOOD JOB

Reflect upon your present blessings—of which every man has many—not on your past misfortunes, of which all men have some.

CHARLES DICKENS

5 Psychology Facts You Should Know:

1. We can udnretsnad any msseed up stnecene as lnog as the lsat and frsit lteerts of wdros are in crrcoet palecs. Suhc as tihs stnecene.

2. Food prepared by someone else tastes much better than your own preparation even when you use the same recipe.

3. In a group setting, people tend to look at the person they feel the closest to when a group laughs.

4. If you sob out of happiness, the first tear will come from the right eye, but if you cry out of sorrow, it will come from the left.

5. People who speak two languages can unintentionally change their personalities when they switch to speak from one language to another.

Useful Habits

Go for a Walk!

Top Benefits:
Improve:
*fitness, posture, mood, circulation
Prevent:
*risk of chronic disease
*fatigue and depression
&
*exposure to sunlight, supports the
body's production of vitamin D.

Relaxing Coloring

"Vikings" Quiz:

1. What is the name of the woman who bore Athelstan's son?

2. Most of the time I'm a joyful man, but I can also be pretty eccentric and even cunning. My loyalty to Ragnar was once questioned and the man who did this lost his life because of his ignorance. So who am I?

3. Once I was a monk, but the Vikings took me as their slave. However, I grew in the eyes of some of them thanks to my ability to adapt to their lifestyle. Yet I have the feeling that Floki doesn't like me at all.

4. What does Floki build that makes him famous?

5. Who is the son of Ragnar and Lagertha?

Crossword Puzzle

Down:

1. zodiac sign
3. product made from soya beans
4. circles a planet
6. academy award
7. home for a bird
8. nationality of Oscar Wilde

Across:

2. Greek cheese
5. kind of whisky
8. land surrounded by water
9. type of book cover
10. kitchen appliance

Want to make a difference?

Kindness ideas

Buy someone a coffee

HAPPY

REFLECTIONS

over last days, weeks, months

Today I feel

Person I cherish and why?

....

....

....

Now, I have courage to:

....

....

....

....

I am brave

FINISH STRONG!

Life has got all those twists
and turns. You've got to hold
on tight and off you go.

Nicole Kidman

Did you know?

What impact has positive thinking on
You

1) Positive thoughts change the structure of the brain.

2) Positivity improves your skill set.

3) Positivity helps you learn.

4) Writing about positivity leads to better health.

5) Positive thinking boosts your immunity.

Useful Habits

READ SOMETHING

Reading Benefits:

1.stimulates growth
2.reduces stress
3.prevents age-related cognitive decline
4.promotes a good night's sleep.
Reading is the workout for your mental health and, the same way you take care of your body, it's important to take care of your brain.

Relaxing Coloring

"Friends" Quiz:

1. How many seasons of Friends are there?
2. Rachel got a job with which company in Paris?
3. What city is Friends set in?
4. Which member of the British royal family appeared on Friends?
5. Ross and Rachel's wedding dinner was held where in Vegas?
6. Phoebe attempts to teach Joey what language?
7. What year did Friends first premiere?

TRICKY QUESTIONS

1.What can one catch that is not thrown?

2.If a plane crashes on the border between the United States and Canada, where do they bury the survivors?

3.Is it legal for a man to marry his widow's sister?

4."The attorney is my brother," testified the accountant. But the attorney testified he did not have a brother. Who is lying?

5.What happened when the wheel was invented?

Want to make a difference?

Kindness ideas

Compliment a parent on their child's behavior

FINAL
REFLECTIONS

over last days, weeks, months

What changes I've noticed during this journey?

_____

_____

_____

_____

PROUD

STRONG   **CALM**   **DETERMINED**

I Feel: **MOTIVATED**   **BRAVE**

GRATEFUL   **OPTIMISTIC**

The end of each journey is the beginning of another one! ;)

What's next?

....

....

....

....

Fantastic job on finishing your
Gratitude Journal!
We would like to say Un Grand Merci
for choosing us as a part of your
journey to a happier life.

Dear Friend,

If you have enjoyed this journal, please take a moment _to leave a review_ with your thoughts and impressions.
We value each opinion and take into consideration every feedback, so that we take a step forward in improving our next creations.
As a new established business, your support is vital for us.

QUIZZES ANSWERS:

Harry Potter Q&A:

1.Name Harry Potter's parents
James and Lily Potter
2.Which actor played the character Cedric Diggory?
Robert Pattinson
3.What creature is Aragog?
Acromantula
4.Who were the four founders of Hogwarts?
Godric Gryffindor, Helga Hufflepuff, Rowena Ravenclaw and Salazar Slytherin
5.What spell would you use to light the tip of your wand?
Lumos

Matrix Q&A:

1.Thomas Anderson is the real name of which character in The Matrix?
Neo
2.A mysterious message on his computer urges Neo to follow which animal?
White Rabbit
3.In The Matrix Reloaded, Neo visits the last city left in the real world. What's its name?
Zion
4.Which piece of technology do awakened humans use to exit the Matrix from inside?
Telephone
5.For what reason is it revealed the machines require farms of humans?
Energy

QUIZZES ANSWERS:

Game of Thrones Q&A:

1.What is the name of Jon's direwolf?

Ghost

2.What is the main religion of the Seven Kingdoms?

Faith of the Seven

3.In the first episode, King Robert Baratheon says "In my dreams, I kill him every night." To whom is the King referring and why?

Rhaegar Targaryen because he kidnapped Lyanna Stark

4.Why could Jon leave the Night's Watch, since his vows were for life?

He died

5. What is the name of Arya Stark's sword?

Needle

Brainteasers Q&A:

1. 84% of people reading this will not find the the mistake in this A,B,C,D,E,F,G,H,I,J,K,L,M,N,O,P,Q,R,S,T,U,V,W,X,Y,Z.

"The" is repeated

2. What flies without wings?

Time

3.What five letter word becomes shorter when you add two letters to it?

The word short

4.What can you keep but cannot share and once you share it, you can't keep it anymore?

A secret

5.What call for help, when written in capital letters, is the same forwards, backwards and upside down?

SOS

QUIZZES ANSWERS:

Vikings Q&A:

1.What is the name of the woman who bore Athelstan's son?

Judith

2. Most of the time I'm a joyful man, but I can also be pretty eccentric and even cunning. My loyalty to Ragnar was once questioned and the man who did this lost his life because of his ignorance. So who am I?

Floki

3. Once I was a monk, but the Vikings took me as their slave. However, I grew in the eyes of some of them thanks to my ability to adapt to their lifestyle. Yet I have the feeling that Floki doesn't like me at all. Who am I?

Athelstan

4.What does Floki build that makes him famous?

Ships

5.Who is the son of Ragnar and Lagertha?

Bjorn

Crossword Puzzle Q&A:

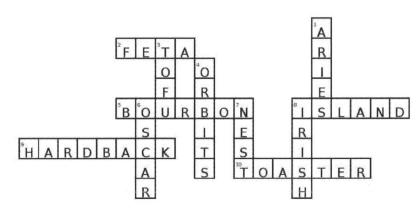

Across:

2. Greek cheese
5. kind of whisky
8. land surrounded by water
9. type of book cover
10. kitchen appliance

Down:

1. zodiac sign
3. product made from soya beans
4. circles a planet
6. academy award
7. home for a bird
8. nationality of Oscar Wilde

QUIZZES ANSWERS:

Friends Q&A:

1.How many seasons of Friends are there?

Ten seasons

2.Rachel got a job with which company in Paris?

Louis Vuitton

3.What city is Friends set in?

New York City

4.Which member of the British royal family appeared on Friends?

Sarah Ferguson/Duchess of York

5.Ross and Rachel's wedding dinner was held where in Vegas?

A Pizza Hut

6.Phoebe attempts to teach Joey what language?

French

7.What year did Friends first premiere?

1994

Tricky Q&A:

1.What can one catch that is not thrown?

A cold

2.If a plane crashes on the border between the United States and Canada, where do they bury the survivors?

Survivors are not buried

3.Is it legal for a man to marry his widow's sister?

No, but since he is dead it would be hard to do so

4."The attorney is my brother," testified the accountant. But the attorney testified he did not have a brother. Who is lying?

None of them was lying if the accountant was a lady

5.What happened when the wheel was invented?

It caused a revolution

Made in the USA
Coppell, TX
17 December 2022

90049307R00072